PICTURE THIS!
Shakespeare

William Shakespe

The Tragedy of Hamlet, Prince of Denmark

EDITED BY
Christina Lacie

ILLUSTRATED BY
Michele Earle-Bridges

BARRON'S

All inquiries should be addressed to:
Barron's Educational Series, Inc.
250 Wireless Boulevard
Hauppauge, New York 11788
www.barronseduc.com

ISBN-13: 978-0-7641-3524-8
ISBN-10: 0-7641-3524-4

Library of Congress Control No.: 2006931423

Printed in China
9 8 7 6 5 4 3

Contents

About the play   iii
Cast of characters or *Dramatis Personae*   iv
Literary terms   vii
Hamlet
Act I   1
Act II   21
Act III   32
Act IV   49
Act V   59

About the play

The Tragedy of Hamlet, Prince of Denmark or *Hamlet* as it is commonly known is a tragedy as its proper name implies. A tragedy is a serious dramatic work in which the audience (or in this case, the reader) witnesses the downfall of the main character otherwise known as the protagonist. The reasons behind the main character's downfall are varied. Perhaps the character is a dreadful decision-maker and is continually making the wrong choices at the right time. Perhaps the character has a flaw in his/her personality that causes him/her to appear weak which then causes him/her to be harshly defeated or as it usually happens in a tragedy, to die. In most of Shakespeare's tragedies however, the main character as well as many other characters, usually die in the final act of the play, which is Act V.

Written in approximately 1600–1601, *Hamlet* is considered one of Shakespeare's best plays. Many believe that it is his best play, yet others believe that *Hamlet* is the greatest tragedy in all of the English language. Whether it is Shakespeare's best play or not, it is definitely his longest play.

Hamlet takes place in Denmark—a small, but powerful country in Scandinavia—located in northern Europe—specifically north of Germany. Hamlet, the main character of the play, is struggling with many family issues: his father, the King of Denmark has recently died, his mother married his father's brother (Hamlet's uncle) within a month of his father's death and Hamlet simply does not understand how she could do such a thing and in such a short period of time.

Early in the play, Hamlet discovers through a visit from his father's ghost that his uncle murdered his father and this is what sets the play into motion. Seeking revenge for his father's death, many characters die in the process, including Hamlet. The play is filled with psychological drama and what comes into question is Hamlet's behavior. Is Hamlet is truly losing his mind or is this behavior simply an act—and he is causing everyone around him to believe that he is insane so that he can revenge his father's murder. Shakespeare's play *Hamlet* is one that will be debated and discussed forever—and as you will discover after reading it, the play will undoubtedly leave you with many questions to consider.

Cast of characters or *Dramatis Personae*

Ghost
Of Hamlet's Father

Hamlet
Prince of Denmark
Son of the late
King Hamlet

Queen Gertrude
Hamlet's Mother
Widow of King
Hamlet and now married
To Claudius

King Claudius
Hamlet's Uncle
and brother to the
late King Hamlet

Ophelia
Daughter of
Polonius

Laertes
Ophelia's Brother

Polonius
Father of Ophelia and
Laertes and councilor to
King Claudius

Reynaldo
Servant to Polonius

Horatio
Hamlet's friend and confidant

Voltemand

Cornelius

Rosencrantz

Guildenstern

Osric

Gentlemen

Courtiers at the Danish Court

A Lord

Francisco

Barnardo

Danish Soldiers/Guards

Marcellus

Fortinbras
Prince
of Norway

A Captain
in Fortinbras's
Army

Ambassadors to Denmark from England

The Prologue   **Player King**   **Player Queen**   **Lucianus**

Actors hired by Hamlet who take on the roles in the play the *Murder of Gonzago*

Messenger   **Messenger**   **Sailor**   **Sailor**

Gravedigger   **Gravedigger's Companion**

Doctor of Divinity

Additional Parts: Attendants, Lords, Guards, Musicians, Laertes' Followers, Soldiers, Officers

Settings of the Scenes:

- Denmark—a small country in Scandinavia, the northern part of Europe
- Outside and within the Castle of Elsinore in Denmark
- A Plain in Denmark
- A Churchyard

Literary terms

alliteration The repetition of one or more beginning sounds, usually consonants, in a group of words.

allusion Referring to historical figures or events, fictional characters, places, or other things that the author assumes the reader will know and understand—for instance, there may be a reference to a myth or to the Bible.

aside When an actor speaks directly to the audience—relaying pertinent information about the character's thoughts or feelings—often called "spoken thoughts" the other characters onstage allegedly do not hear what is said.

foreshadowing Hints or clues that prepare the reader for something that might happen later in the work.

hyperbole Language that greatly overstates or exaggerates for rhetorical or comic effect.

iambic pentameter A line of verse that has ten syllables, rhymed or unrhymed—unstressed and stressed.

irony Term indicating a difference between what appears to be true and what actually is true.

metaphor A figure of speech that compares unlike objects without using connecting terms such as *like* or *as*.

metonymy A figure of speech that substitutes a word or a phrase for another that it is associated with, for instance, the word *Norway* is used to refer to the governing body or the King of Norway in Act 1, scene ii.

oxymoron A statement that combines two terms usually seen as opposites. The effect created seems to be a contradiction, but is true. Some examples are *deafening silence, jumbo shrimp*.

personification A figure of speech in which objects or animals are given human qualities.

pun A play on words that has more than one meaning.

simile A figurative comparison using the words *like* or *as*. Some examples are *pretty as a picture, cunning like a fox*.

soliloquy A speech given in a drama, when characters speak their thoughts aloud while alone on stage, thereby communicating their thoughts, mental state, intentions, and motives to the audience.

symbolism Something that stands for or can mean something else. For example, in Act I, scene ii— Hamlet's uncle asks: "How is it that the clouds still hang on you?" Clouds are symbolic of something sad or dark that hovers over someone or something.

tragedy A form of literature in which the hero is destroyed by a character flaw and a set of forces that cause the hero considerable suffering. *Hamlet* is an example of a tragedy, as is *Romeo and Juliet, King Lear, Macbeth,* and *Othello*.

Many examples of these terms have been pointed out for you throughout this book. Pay attention and you may find even more!

<table>
<tr><td>**Act I
Scene i**</td><td>Francisco greets Barnardo followed by the arrival of Marcellus and Horatio. Horatio asks about the ghost of King Hamlet seen during their watch.</td></tr>
</table>

Who's there?

Stand and identify yourself!

Long live the King!

Good night

'Tis now struck twelve. Get thee to bed, Francisco.

Welcome, Horatio— Welcome, good Marcellus.

Holla, Barnardo

Sit down and let us **assail** your ears with what we have two nights seen.

Has this thing appeared again tonight?

Think About It

What are your thoughts about ghosts? Are they real? Are they a figment of our imagination? Or, are ghosts the creations that appear on Halloween and that's it?

assail—attack or assault

1

Marcellus and Barnardo explain to Horatio that they have seen an **apparition** when the ghost of the dead King Hamlet suddenly appears. They beg Horatio to speak to it, but it disappears.

Last night when the bell beat one, Marcellus and myself . . .

Peace! Look where it comes again. Thou art a **scholar**. Speak to it, Horatio.

It **harrows** me with fear and wonder.

Speak to it Horatio!

What are you that **usurp'st** this time of night, with the warlike form of the buried king of Denmark. Speak! Stay! Speak! Speak!

See, it stalks away.

apparition—ghost, spirit   **scholar**—one who best knows how to speak to or approach something
harrows—distresses, torments
usurp'st—to take power

2

Marcellus: Good now, sit down, and tell me, he that knows,
Why this same strict and most observant watch
So nightly toils the subject of the land,
And why such daily cast of **brazen** cannon
And **foreign mart** for implements of war,
Why such impress of shipwrights, whose sore task
Does not divide the Sunday from the week.
What might be toward that this sweaty haste
Doth make the night joint laborer with the day?
Who is't that can inform me?

Horatio: That can I.
At least the whisper goes so: our last king,
Was, as you know, by Fortinbras of Norway,
Dared to the combat; in which our valiant Hamlet
Did slay this Fortinbras, who by a sealed compact,
Well ratified by law and **heraldry**
Did forfeit, with his life, all his lands
Which he stood seized of, to the conqueror.
Now, young Fortinbras,
Of **unimproved mettle** hot and full,
Hath in the skirts of Norway here and there
Sharked up a list of lawless resolutes
For food and diet to some enterprise
That hath a stomach in't; which is no other
But to recover of us, by strong hand
And terms compulsatory, those foresaid lands
So by his father lost. And this, I take it,
Is the main motive of our preparations,
The source of this our watch, and the chief head
Of this posthaste and rummage in the land.

brazen—cannons made of brass
foreign mart—international trade

Think About It
Young Fortinbras is angry not only about the death of his father, but he wants to regain the lands that were lost to Denmark. Can you blame him? Would you agree that Fortinbras is seeking revenge?

heraldry—laws regulating battles and tournaments

unimproved mettle—uncontrolled anger

Barnardo questions as to why the Ghost would appear during their watch. Horatio responds that perhaps the Ghost is warning Denmark of dangerous times ahead.

Barnardo: I think it be not other but **e'en** so.
Well may it sort that this portentous figure
Comes armed through our watch so like the king
That was and is the question of these wars.

Literary Terms
Shakespeare uses **contractions**, like *e'en*, to maintain the **iambic** count of 10 syllables per line.

Horatio: A **mote** it is to trouble the mind's eye.
In the most high and palmy state of Rome,
A little ere the mightiest **Julius** fell,
The graves stood tenantless, and the sheeted dead
Did squeak and gibber in the Roman streets;
As stars with trains of fire and dews of blood,
Disasters in the sun; and the **moist star**,
Upon whose influence **Neptune's** empire stands,
Was sick almost to **doomsday** with **eclipse**.
And even the like precurse of [feared] events,
As **harbingers** preceding still the fates
And prologue to the omen coming on,
Have heaven and earth together demonstrated
Unto our climatures and countrymen.

mote—speck of dust

Julius [Caesar]—the murdered ruler/dictator of ancient Rome

moist star—the moon which influences the tides
Neptune's—Neptune was the god of the sea
doomsday—a Biblical allusion referring to the end of the world
harbingers—advance messengers

Literary Terms
These are common **allusions** to historic figures, mythology, the Bible, and other events that would be familiar to those watching one of Shakespeare's plays

As Horatio explains the Ghost's presence, it reappears, but with the crowing of a rooster it again disappears. The men decide to tell young Hamlet about their experience.

Behold! It comes again! Stay illusion! **"If thou art privy to thy country's fate, O, speak!"**

Shall I strike it with my **partisan**?

Do, if it will not stand.

'Tis gone.

It was about to speak when the cock crew.

It faded on the crowing of the cock.

Let us tell Hamlet what we have seen; for upon my life, this spirit, **dumb** to us, will speak to him.

"If thou art privy . . . speak"—it was common belief in Shakespeare's time that there were four reasons why the spirit of a dead man would walk.

1) to reveal a secret
2) to utter a warning
3) to reveal a hidden treasure
4) to reveal the way it died

partisan—a spear-like weapon
dumb—will not or cannot speak

King

Though yet of Hamlet our dear brother's death
The memory be **green**, and that it us befitted
To bear our hearts in grief, and our whole kingdom
To be contracted in one brow of woe,
Yet so far hath discretion fought with nature
That we with wisest sorrow think on him
Together with remembrance of ourselves.
Therefore our sometime sister, now our queen,
Th'imperial **jointress** to this warlike state,
Have we (as 'twere with a defeated joy,
With an auspicious and a dropping eye,
With mirth in funeral and with dirge in marriage,
In equal scale weighing delight and dole)
Taken to wife. Nor have we herein barred
Your better wisdoms, which have freely gone
With this affair along. For all, our thanks.
Now follows that you know. Young Fortinbras,
Holding a weak supposal of our worth
Or thinking by our late dear brother's death
Our state to be disjoint and out of frame,
Colleaguèd with this dream of his advantage,
He hath not failed to pester us with message
Importing the surrender of those lands
Lost by his father, with all bonds of law,
To our most valiant brother—so much for him.

Literary Terms

A **metaphor**, such as **memory be green**, is used to state that the memory of the death is fresh in their minds.

Think About It

There is a great deal going on at this time—grieving over the death of King Hamlet, the celebration of the marriage of King Claudius and Queen Gertrude, and the possibility of a battle with Young Fortinbras who wants to regain the lands Norway lost in battle.

jointress—a woman who owns property with her husband
with an auspicious and dropping eye—one eye open and smiling—the other eye sad and closed

<table>
<tr><td>**Act I
Scene ii**</td><td>King Claudius asks Cornelius and Voltemand to deliver a letter to the King of Norway explaining that Denmark is prepared to retaliate if young Fortinbras attacks.</td></tr>
</table>

We have written to **Norway**, uncle of young Fortinbras, of his nephew's plan and we send you to **business** with the King.

Literary Terms

When the King refers to writing to **Norway**, he means to the **King of Norway**—this is known as **metonymy**

Farewell, and let your haste commend your duty.

In that and all things will we show our duty

business—to negotiate with

King Claudius grants Laertes permission to return to France. Both the Queen and King question Hamlet about his sadness.

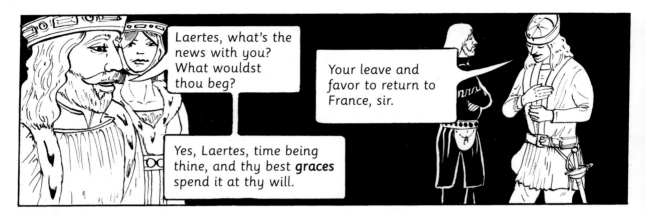

Laertes, what's the news with you? What wouldst thou beg?

Your leave and favor to return to France, sir.

Yes, Laertes, time being thine, and thy best **graces** spend it at thy will.

But now, my cousin Hamlet and my son—how is it that **the clouds still hang on you?**

A little more than **kin** and less than kind.

Literary Terms:

Symbolism—clouds are symbolic for something dark or sad that hovers over a person or situation. Using an **aside** Hamlet states that he is more than related or "kin"—because he is a nephew and now a son—and "less than kind" a relationship with little natural affection.

Good Hamlet, cast thy **nighted** color off. It is common that all that lives must die.

Ay, Madam, it is common.

graces—permission   **kin**—a relative   **nighted**—dark as in night

8

Hamlet responds angrily to his mother's question about his sadness. The King states that everyone loses a father and that Hamlet should not return to school in Wittenberg, Germany.

Queen: Why seems it [sadness] so particular with thee?

Hamlet: "Seems," madam? Nay, it is. I know not "seems,"
'Tis not alone my **inky cloak**, good mother,
Nor customary suits of solemn black,
Nor **windy suspiration of forced breath**,
No, nor the **fruitful river** in the eye,
Nor the **dejected havior of the visage**,
Together with all forms, moods, shapes of grief,
That can denote me truly. These "seem,"
For they are actions that a man might play;
But I have that within which passes show,
These but the trappings and the suits of woe.

King: 'Tis sweet and commendable in your nature, Hamlet,
To give these mourning duties to your father.
But you must know your father lost a father,
That father lost, lost his, and the survivor bound
In filial obligation for some term
To do **obsequious sorrow**. But to persevere
In **obstinate condolement** is a course
Of **impious stubbornness**. 'Tis unmanly grief.
We pray you, throw to earth
This unprevailing woe and think of us.
For your intent
In going back to school in Wittenberg,
It is most retrograde to our desire,
And we beseech you, bend you to remain
Here in the cheer and comfort of our eye . . .

Queen: I pray thee, stay with us. Go not to Wittenberg.

Hamlet: I shall in all my best obey you, madam.

> **Think About It**
> Although his parents seem concerned about him—and want Hamlet to shake off his sadness—wouldn't sending him back to school be a good thing? Or not? Revisit this question when you have finished reading the play.

inky cloak— dark clothes worn in mourning   **windy suspiration of forced breath**—audible sighs
fruitful river—tears from crying   **dejected havior of the visage**—sadness that shows on a person's face
obsequious sorrow—dutiful sadness or mourning
obstinate condolment—sorrow that refuses to be comforted   **impious stubbornness**—refusing to give in

O, that this too, too sullied flesh would melt,
Thaw, and resolve itself into a dew,
Or that the **Everlasting** had not fixed
His canon **'gainst self-slaughter**! O God, God,
How weary, stale, flat and unprofitable
Seem to me all the uses of this world!
Fie on't, ah fie! "Tis an unweeded garden
That grows to seed. Things rank and gross in nature
Possess it merely. That it should come to this:
But two months dead—nay, not so much, not two.
So excellent a king, that was to this
Hyperion to a satyr; so loving to my mother
That he might not beteem the winds of heaven
Visit her face too roughly. Heaven and earth!
Must I remember?" Why, she would hang on him
As if increase of appetite had grown
By what it fed on. And yet, within a month
Let me not think on't: **frailty, thy name is woman**!,
A little month, or ere those shoes were old
With which she followed my poor father's body,
Like **Niobe**, all tears—why she, even she
O God, a beast that wants discourse of reason
Would have mourned longer!, married with my uncle,
My father's brother, but no more like my father
Than I to **Hercules**. Within a month,
Ere yet the salt of most unrighteous tears
Had left the flushing in her **galled** eyes,
She married. O, most wicked speed, to post
With such dexterity to incestuous sheets!
It is not, nor it cannot come to good.
But break, my heart, for I must hold my tongue.

Everlasting—God
'gainst self-slaughter—against suicide
galled—injured by tears

Literary Terms

In a **soliloquy**, Hamlet compares **Hyperion** the sun god, to a satyr—a goat-like creature which is an **allusion**.

A well-known quote—**frailty** is weakness in a physical and moral sense.

Literary Term

In Greek mythology, **Niobe's** children were killed, and she cried so much that she was turned into a stone from which water flowed continually. This is an **allusion**.

Literary Term

An **allusion** to Greek mythology is the reference to **Hercules**; a hero of extraordinary strength and courage.

Act I Scene ii	Horatio, Marcellus and Barnardo approach Hamlet and tell him that they have seen the ghost of his father. Hamlet decides to stand watch with them that evening.

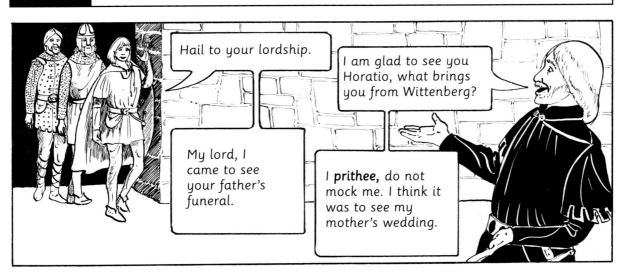

Hail to your lordship.

I am glad to see you Horatio, what brings you from Wittenberg?

My lord, I came to see your father's funeral.

I **prithee,** do not mock me. I think it was to see my mother's wedding.

My lord, two nights together and with me the third, have on their watch, encountered a figure like your father **armed**.

'Tis very strange. I will watch tonight. Perchance 'twill walk again and I'll speak to it. Fare you well. Upon the platform, 'twixt eleven and twelve, I'll visit you.

Think About It

If you could speak to the spirit of someone—who would it be and why? What would you like to ask? What would you want to discuss?

prithee—a form of "pray thee"
armed—wearing battle armor

11

Act I Scene iii	Laertes offers brotherly advice to his sister Ophelia regarding Hamlet. Their father Polonius enters and gives Laertes some fatherly advice.

Farewell, and as for Hamlet, hold his attentions as **a violet in the youth of primy nature**, not permanent, sweet, not lasting, the perfume and suppliance of a minute, no more.

I shall the effect of this good lesson keep as watchman to my heart.

Polonius: There, my blessing with thee.
And these few precepts in thy memory
Look thou character. **Give thy thoughts no tongue,**
Nor any unproportioned thought his act.
Be thou familiar, but by no means vulgar.
Those friends thou hast, and their adoption tried,
Grapple them unto thy soul with hoops of steel,
But do not dull thy palm with entertainment
Of each new-hatched, unfledged courage. Beware
Of entrance to a quarrel, but, being in,
Bear't that th'opposèd may beware of thee.
Give everyman thy ear, but few thy voice.
Take each man's censure, but reserve thy judgment
Costly thy habit as thy purse can buy,
But not expressed in fancy (rich, not gaudy),
For the apparel oft proclaims the man,
And they in France of the best rank and station
Are of a most select and generous chief in that
Neither a borrower nor a lender be,
For loan oft loses both itself and friend,
And borrowing dulls the edge of husbandry.
This above all; to thine own self be true,
And it must follow, as the night the day,
Thou canst not then be false to any man.
Farewell. My blessing season this in thee.

a violet in the youth of primy nature—in early days of its prime

Think About It

These are notable sayings from the Polonius character—note his advice to his son Laertes. What does this advice mean to you? Is it good advice or not?

Act I Scene iii	As Laertes leaves, he reminds Ophelia of their conversation. Curious, Polonius questions Ophelia, then offers fatherly advice, and forbids Ophelia to see Hamlet.

Farewell Ophelia, and remember well what I have said to you.

'Tis in my memory locked, and you yourself shall keep the key of it.

What is't Ophelia, he hath said to you?

'I have been told that Hamlet has given private time to you, and you have of your **audience** been most free and bounteous. What is between you? Give me up the truth.

So please you, something touching the Lord Hamlet.

He hath, my lord, of late made many tenders of his affection to me.

Affection, puh! **You speak like a green girl.** Do not believe his vows. This is for all: I would not, in plain terms from this time on to give any moment leisure as to words or talk with the Lord Hamlet. Look to't, I charge you.

I shall obey, my lord.

Literary Terms
Shakespeare uses a **simile** by referring to Ophelia's manner as inexperienced or "green."

audience—accompany, to be with someone
You speak like a green girl—**(simile—see literary terms page)**—you speak as one who is very young and inexperienced

Hamlet, Horatio and Marcellus are on the watch platform and the ghost appears and signals for Hamlet to follow.

Look, my lord, it comes.

Angels and **ministers of grace**, defend us! Be thou a spirit of health or goblin damned, thou cometh in such a shape that I will speak to thee. I'll call thee "Hamlet," "King," "Father," "Royal Dane." O answer me!

It beckons you to go away with it. Do not my lord.

My fate cries out and makes each petty **arture** in this body as hardy as the **Nemean lion's nerve**. Still am I called. Unhand me, gentlemen. I say, away! Go on. I'll follow thee.

Look with what courteous action it waves you to a more removed ground. But do not go with it.

Literary Term

An **allusion** is used to compare the arteries in Hamlet's body to those of the fierce lion killed by Hercules.

ministers of grace—servants or messengers of God, angels
arture—arteries which were believed to carry the body's invisible spirits.

14

Horatio: He **waxes** desperate with imagination.

Marcellus: Let's follow. 'Tis not fit thus to obey him.

Horatio: Have after. To what issue will this come?

Marcellus: **Something is rotten in the state of Denmark.**

Horatio: Heaven will direct it.

Marcellus: Nay, let's follow him.

Think About It—

Something is rotten in the state of Denmark is one of the most noted quotes in all of English literature. Have you ever heard of it or used it in one way or another? What do you suppose this quote means?

waxes—to grow or increase

**Act I
Scene v**

Hamlet leaves with the ghost of his father and the ghost tells
Hamlet that if he ever did love him that he will revenge his murder.

Ghost: I am thy father's spirit,
Doomed for a certain term to walk the night
And for the day confined to fast in fires
Till the foul crimes done in my days of nature
Are burnt and purged away. But that I am forbid
To tell the secrets of my prison house,
I could a tale unfold whose lightest word
Would harrow up thy soul, freeze thy young blood,
Make thy two eyes, like stars, start from their spheres,
Thy knotted and combined **locks** to part,
And each particular hair to stand on end,
Like quills upon the fearful porpentine.
But this eternal blazon must not be
To ears of flesh and blood. **List**, list, O list!
If thou didst ever thy dear father love—

Think About It

Notice the description
that the ghost uses to
describe the "secrets
of his prison house."

Hamlet: O God!

Ghost: Revenge his foul and most unnatural
murder.

Hamlet: Murder?

Ghost: Murder most foul, as in the best it is,
But this most foul, strange, and unnatural.

sul'frous—applied to the flames of hell
locks—a tuft of hair   **list**—listen

| Act I Scene v | The ghost tells Hamlet that although Denmark was told that he was killed by a serpent—in truth, his brother (now King Claudius) put poison in his ears while he was napping in the orchard. |

Now, Hamlet, 'Tis given out that, sleeping in my orchard, a serpent stung me. The whole ear of Denmark is misled. But know, the serpent that did sting thy father's life now wears his crown.

O, my prophetic soul! My uncle!

Ghost: Ay, that **incestuous**, that adulterate beast,
With witchcraft of his wit, with traitorous gifts—
O wicked wit and gifts, that have the power
So to seduce! –won to his shameful lust
The will of my most seeming-virtuous queen.
O Hamlet, what a falling off was there!
From me, whose love was of that dignity
That it went hand in hand even with the vow
I made to her in marriage, and to decline
Upon a wretch whose natural gifts were poor
To those of mine.
But virtue, as it never will be moved,
Though lewdness court it in a shape of heaven,
So, lust, though to a radiant angel linked,
Will sate itself in a **celestial** bed
And prey on garbage.
But soft, methinks I scent the morning air.
Brief let me be. Sleeping within my orchard,
My custom always of the afternoon,
Upon my secure hour thy uncle stole,
With **juice of cursed hebona** in a vial,
And in the porches of my ears did pour
The leprous distilment, whose effect
Holds such an enmity with blood of man
That swift as **quicksilver** it courses through

The natural gates and alleys of the body,
And with a sudden vigor it doth **posset**
And curd, like eager droppings into milk,
The thin and wholesome blood. So did it mine,
And a most instant tetter barked about,
Most lazar-like, with vile and loathsome crust
All my smooth body.
Thus was I, sleeping, by a brother's hand
Of life, of crown, of queen at once dispatched,
Cut off, even in the blossoms of my sin,
Unhouseled, disappointed, unaneled,
No reck'ning made, but sent to my account
With all my imperfections on my head.
O horrible, O horrible, most horrible!
If thou hast nature in thee, bear it not.
Let not the royal bed of Denmark be
A couch for luxury and damnèd incest.
But, howsomever thou pursues this act,
Taint not thy mind, nor let thy soul contrive
Against thy mother aught. Leave her to heaven
And to those thorns that in her bosom lodge
To prick and sting her. Fare thee well at once.
The glowworm shows the **matin** to be near
And 'gins to pale his uneffectual fire
Adieu, adieu, adieu. Remember me.

incestuous—sexual commerce unpermitted by the law   **celestial**—heavenly
juice of cursed hebona—probably ebony—the liquid from which was thought to be poisonous
quicksilver—mercury, emblem of swiftness   **posset**—to curdle   **matin**—morning

O all you host of heaven! O earth! What else?
And shall I couple hell? O fie! Hold, hold, my heart,
And you, my sinews, grow not instant old,
But bear me stiffly up. Remember thee?
Ay, thou poor ghost, whiles memory holds a seat
In this **distracted globe**. Remember thee?
Yea, from the table of my memory
I'll wipe away all trivial, fond records,
All **saws** of books, all forms, all pressures past,
That youth and observation copied there,
And thy commandment all alone shall live
Within the book and volume of my brain,
Unmixed with baser matter. Yes, by heaven!
O most **pernicious** woman!
O villain, villain, smiling, damnèd villain!
At least I am sure it may be so in Denmark.
            (He writes)
So, uncle, there you are. Now to my word.
It is "adieu, adieu, remember me."
I have sworn't.

Think About It

Have you ever been given startling news? If so, how did you react? Were you calm— or did you overreact? How do you handle stressful situations?

distracted globe—mad out of one's senses (**globe** refers to brain/head)
saws—a moral saying
pernicious—mischievous or malicious

Act I Scene v	Horatio and Marcellus find Hamlet and are excited to hear about his encounter. He asks them to promise that they will never reveal what they saw tonight.

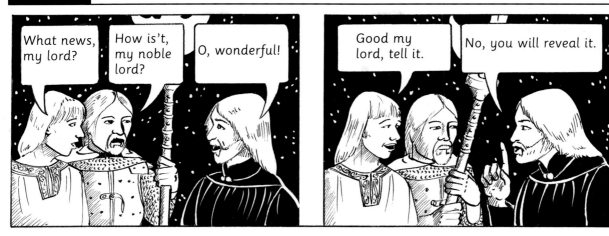

What news, my lord?

How is't, my noble lord?

O, wonderful!

Good my lord, tell it.

No, you will reveal it.

Not I, my lord, by heaven.

Nor I, my lord.

But you'll be secret? There's never a villain dwelling in all Denmark but he's an **arrant** knave. I hold it fit that we shake hands and part, you, as your business shall point you, and for my part, I will go pray.

These are but wild and **whirling** words, my lord.

I am sorry they offend you, and yes by **Saint Patrick**, but there is much offense too. Good friends, give me one poor request. Never make known what you have seen tonight.

arrant—complete and total   **whirling**—giddy
Saint Patrick—the patron saint of Ireland—it is said that he cast out the snakes all over the country

Hamlet, with the support of the ghost, demands that Horatio and Marcellus swear that they will not reveal what they have seen or heard tonight.

Hamlet: Indeed upon my sword, indeed.

Ghost: *(cries from under the stage)* Swear.

Hamlet: Ha, ha, boy, sayst thou so? Art thou there, **truepenny**?
Come on, you hear this fellow in the cellarage.
Consent to swear.

truepenny—honest person

Horatio: Propose the oath, my lord.

Hamlet: Never to speak of this that you have seen,
Swear by my sword.

Ghost: *(beneath)* Swear.

Hamlet: Lay your hands again upon my sword.
Swear by my sword
Never to speak of this that you have heard.

Ghost: *(beneath)* Swear by his sword.

Hamlet: Well said, old mole. Canst work i'th'earth so fast?
Once more remove, good friends.

Horatio: O day and night, but this is wondrous strange.

Hamlet: And therefore as a stranger give it welcome.
But come, here, as before, never, so help you mercy,
How strange or odd some'er I bear myself
(As I perchance hereafter shall think meet
To put an antic disposition on)
That you, at such times seeing me, never shall,
With arm encumbered thus, or this headshake,
Or by pronouncing of some doubtful phrase,
That you know aught of me—this do swear,
So grace and mercy at your most need help you.

Ghost: *(beneath)* Swear.

Hamlet: Rest, rest, perturbèd spirit.—So, gentlemen,
With all my love I do commend me to you,
And what so poor a man as Hamlet is
May do't express his love and friendling to you,
God willing, shall not lack. Let us go in together,
And still your fingers on your lips, I pray.
The time is out of joint. O cursèd spite
That ever I was born to set it right!

> **Literary Terms**
>
> Hamlet is preparing Horatio and Marcellus for his possible erratic and unusual behavior in the future—this is known as **foreshadowing**.

> **Think About It**
>
> One of the most debated aspects of the play *Hamlet* is Hamlet's sanity. Is this all a show as it seems to be foreshadowed here, or does Hamlet sincerely lose his mind?

Polonius sends Reynaldo to Paris to check on Laertes. Ophelia appears and is extremely troubled by a disturbing visit from Hamlet.

Give him this money and notes. But, before you visit him inquire of his behavior, who his friends are and how he spends his money.

Good my lord. I shall, my lord.

Polonius: How now Ophelia, what's the matter?

Ophelia: O, my lord, my lord, I have been so affrighted!
As I was in my sewing closet,
Lord Hamlet, with his doublet unbraced,
No hat upon his head, his stockings fouled,
Ungartered, and down-gyved to his ankle,
Pale as his shirt, his knees knocking each other,
And with a look so piteous in purpose
As if he had been loosed out of hell
To speak of horrors—he comes before me.

Polonius: Mad for thy love?

Ophelia: My lord, I do not know, but truly I do fear it.

Polonius: What said he?

Ophelia: He took me by the wrist and held me hard
Then goes he to the length of all his arm,
And, with his other hand thus o'er his brow,
He falls to such perusal of my face
As he would draw it. Long stayed he so.
He raised a sigh so piteous and profound
As it did seem to shatter all his bulk
And end his being. That done he lets me go.

Polonius: Come, go with me. I will go seek the King.
This is the very ecstasy of love . . . I am sorry.
What, have you given him any hard words of late?

Ophelia: No, but as you did command
I did repel his letters and denied his access to me.

Polonius: That hath made him mad.
Come, go we to the King. This must be known, come.

Think About It

Ophelia's description of Hamlet's appearance sounds as if he'd seen a ghost—his jacket undone, no hat, his stockings falling to his ankles, knees knocking and as pale as his shirt—(we assume it is white). What do you think?

The King and Queen welcome Hamlet's friends Rosencrantz and Guildenstern whom they have invited to both spy on and to cheer Hamlet.

Welcome, we long to see you—have you heard of Hamlet's transformation?

Good gentlemen, your visitation shall receive such thanks as fits a king's remembrance.

Thanks, and I entreat you both to draw him on to pleasures and to gather aught to us unknown, what afflicts him.

Thanks, and I beseech you instantly to visit my too much changed son.

Might you put your dread pleasures more into command than to entreaty.

We both obey, and lay our service at your feet.

The ambassadors from Norway are returned.

Thou hast been the father of good news.

And, I assure my good lord, I have found the very cause of Hamlet's lunacy.

But, give first admittance to the ambassadors.

O, speak, I long to hear, but do grace to them and bring them in.

Think About It

Hamlet's mother certainly must be concerned about her son's mental state. What might she believe to be the source of Hamlet's changed mental condition?

Voltemand reports to the king about Fortinbras' army and the plans to attack the Polish and not the Danes.

King: Welcome my good friends. Say Voltemand, what from our brother Norway?

Voltemand: Most fair return of greetings and desires.
Upon our first meeting, he sent out to suppress
His nephew's **levies**, which to him appeared
To be a preparation 'gainst the Polack,
But better looked into, he found
It was against your Highness. Whereat, grieved
That so his sickness, age, and impotence
Was falsely borne in hand, sends out arrests
On Fortinbras, which he, obeys,
Receives **rebuke** from Norway, and, in fine,
Makes vow before his uncle never more
To give th'assay of arms against your Majesty.
Whereon old Norway, overcome with joy,
Gives him three-score thousand crowns in annual fee
And his commission to employ those soldiers,
So levied as before, against the Polack,
With an entreaty, herein further shown *(he hands the King a letter)*
That it might please you to give quiet pass
Through your dominions for this enterprise,
On such regards of safety and allowance
As therein are set down.

levies—gathering an army together for war

rebuke—to stop or restrain

King: It likes us well,
And, at our more considered time, we'll read,
Answer, and think upon this business.
Meantime, we thank you for your well-took labor.
Go to your rest. At night we'll feast together.
Most welcome home!

Think About It

The King now believes that Fortinbras is intending to peacefully march through Denmark in order to attack the Poles. If you were King, would you trust the word of "old Norway" or would you be suspicious of a young man (Fortinbras) who like Hamlet, lost his father and might be agreeing not to attack Denmark just to appease his elderly and sick uncle.

Polonius: My liege and madam, to expostulate
What majesty should be, what duty is,
Why day is day, night night, and time is time
Were nothing but to waste night, day, and time.
Therefore, **since brevity is the soul of wit**,
And tediousness the limbs and outward flourishes
I will be brief. Your noble son is mad.
"Mad" call I it, for, to define true madness,
What is't but to be nothing else but mad?

Queen: More matter with less art.

Polonius: Madam, I swear I use no art at all.
That he's mad, 'tis true; 'tis true 'tis pity,
And pity 'tis 'tis true—a foolish figure,
But farewell it, for I will use no art.
That we find out the cause of this effect,
Or, rather say, the cause of this defect,
For this effect defective come by cause.
Perpend.
I have a daughter (have while she is mine)
Who, in her duty and obedience,
Hath given me this.
(He reads) To the celestial, and my soul's idol, the most beautified Ophelia—
That's an ill phrase, a vile phrase; "beautified"
is a vile phrase. But you shall hear. Thus: *(He continues to read)*
    In her excellent white bosom, these, etc.—
    Doubt thou the stars are fire, Doubt that the sun doth move,
    Doubt truth to be a liar, But never doubt I love.
    O dear Ophelia, I am ill at these numbers. I have not
    Art to reckon my groans, but that I love thee best, O
    most best, believe it. Adieu
        Thine evermore, most dear lady, whilst
            this machine is to him, Hamlet.

Queen: Came this from Hamlet to her?

King: But how hath she received his love?

> ### Think About It
> Polonius seems to understand that **"Brevity is the soul of wit"** (another of Polonius' notable statements) and that being brief is the "soul" of intellectual power, but yet he continues to ramble when he speaks.

Perpend—consider carefully

Polonius finally gets to the point in explaining Hamlet's madness and then plans to watch Hamlet with Ophelia to prove it.

Polonius: When I had seen this hot love on the wing,
What might you, or my dear Majesty your queen here, think,
If I had played the desk or table-book
Or given my heart a (winking,) mute and dumb,
Or looked upon this love with idle sight?
What might you think? No, I went round to work,
And my young mistress thus I did bespeak:
"Lord Hamlet is a prince, out of thy star.
This must not be." And then I ordered,
That she should lock herself from (his) resort,
Admit no messengers, receive not tokens;
Which done, she took the fruits of my advice,
And he, repelled,
Fell into a sadness, then into a fast,
Thence to a watch, thence into a weakness,
Thence to a lightness, and, by this declension,
Into the madness wherein now he raves
And we all mourn for.

Think About It

Does Polonius propose setting Hamlet up by using Ophelia as a decoy?

Act II Scene ii	Polonius attempts to have a conversation with Hamlet, but Hamlet responds with what seems to be nonsense.

Do you know me my Lord?

Excellent well. You are a fishmonger.

Not I, my lord.

Then I would you were so honest a man.

What do you read my lord?

Words, words, words. Slanders, sir; for the satirical rogue says here that old men have gray beards, that their faces are wrinkled, their eyes purging thick amber and plum-tree gum, and that they have a plentiful lack of wit...

Though this be madness, yet there is method in't.

Fare you well, my lord.

These tedious old fools.

Think About It

Have you ever heard someone say— there is method in his (or her or my) madness? This is yet another infamous quote from the play. Is Polonius suspicious of Hamlet at this point? What is the method or reason for Hamlet acting insane?

Rosencrantz and Guildenstern arrive. Hamlet briefly questions the two and then tells them the reasons the King and Queen sent for them.

My excellent good friends, what make you at Elsinore? Were you not sent for? Is it your own inclining?

To visit you, my lord.

Alas, my lord, we were sent for.

I will tell you why; I have of late, but wherefore I know not, lost all my mirth, forgone all custom of exercises, and, indeed it goes so heavily with my disposition that this goodly frame, the earth, seems to me a sterile promontory; this most excellent canopy, the air, this majestical roof, why, it appears nothing to me but a foul and pestilent congregation of vapors. **What a piece of work is a man**, how noble in reason, how infinite in faculties, in form and moving how express and admirable; in action how like an angel, in apprehension how like a god; the beauty of the world, the paragon of animals—and yet, to me, what is this quintessence of dust? Man delights not me, no, nor women neither—

Think About It

Hamlet is happy to see his friends, but suspicious of why they are in Elsinore. His statement—"What a piece of work is a man" is also a noted quote. What does it mean and how does it apply to the present situation between his parents and friends?

Hamlet re-welcomes his friends and tells them that his mother and uncle are deceived about his insanity, because he states that he is only insane part of the time.

Gentlemen, welcome to Elsinore. Your hand, th' appurtenance of welcome is fashion and ceremony. You are welcome. But my uncle-father and aunt-mother are deceived.

In what, my dear lord?

I am but mad north-north-west. When the wind is southerly, I **know a hawk from a handsaw.**

Literary Term

A **proverb** is used here to express the fact that Hamlet knows the difference between two unlike things—a hawk and a handsaw—but truthfully, he is aware of when he is sane and when he is seemingly insane.

<table>
<tr><td>**Act II Scene ii**</td><td>A troop of actors arrive. Hamlet asks them to retell the speech about Aeneus and the Fall of Troy and to perform the *Murder of Gonzago*.</td></tr>
</table>

My lord, the actors are come hither. The best actors in the world.

Welcome masters; welcome all. I am glad to see thee well. We'll have a speech straight—come give us a passionate speech of Aeneus and Priam's slaughter.

Anon he finds him striking too short at Greeks. His antique sword, rebellious to his arm, lies where it falls, repugnant to command...

'Tis well. We'll hear a play tomorrow night—can you play "The Murder of Gonzago"? You could for a need, study a speech of some dozen or sixteen lines which I would set down and insert, could you not?

Ay, my lord.

Think About It

Aeneas' tale of the slaughter of Prium comes from the ancient Greek author's epic poem titled *Aeneid*. It tells of the death of the king of Troy, Priam (who was killed by Pyrrhus) while seeking revenge for his father's (Achilles) death. Why would Hamlet request **this** story from the actor? Can you see any parallels with Hamlet's situation?

Now I am alone.
O, what a rogue and peasant slave am I!
Is it not monstrous that this player here,
But in a fiction, in a dream of passion, Could
force his soul so to his own conceit
That from her working all his visage waned,
Tears in his eye, distraction in his aspect,
A broken voice, and his whole function suiting
With forms to his conceit—and all for nothing!
For **Hecuba!**
What's Hecuba to him or he to Hecuba,? That he
should weep for her? What would he do
Had he the motive and the cue for passion
That I have? He would drown the stage in tears
And cleave the general ear with horrid speech,
Make mad the guilty and appall the free,
Confound the ignorant and amaze indeed
The very faculties of eyes and ears. Yet I
A dull and muddy-meddled rascal, peak
Like John-a-dreams, unpregnant of my cause,
And can say nothing—no not for a king
Upon whose property and most dear life
A damned defeat was made. . . .
 (O, vengeance!)
Why, what an ass am I! This is most brave,
That I, the son of a dear father murdered,
Prompted to my revenge by heaven and hell,
Must, like a whore, unpack my heart with words
And fall a-cursing like a very drab,
A scullion! Fie upon't! Foh!
About my brains!—Hum, I have heard

That guilty creatures sitting at a play
Have, by the very cunning of the scene,
Been struck so to the soul that presently
They have proclaimed their malefactions.
For murder, though it have no tongue, will speak
With most miraculous organ.
I'll have these players
Play something like the murder of my father
Before mine uncle. I'll observe his looks;
I'll tent him to the quick. If he do blench,
I know my course. The spirit that I have seen
May be a devil, and the devil hath power
T'assume a pleasing shape; yea, and perhaps,
Out of my weakness and my melancholy,
As he is very potent with such spirits,
Abuses me to damn me. I'll have grounds
More relative than this. **The play's the thing**
Wherein I'll catch the conscience of the King.

Think About It

Hamlet believes that **"the play's the thing,"** that he will expose Claudius' guilt through the emotions and talents of the actors on the stage. Is the [play] the thing? When you watch a film or a play, do you ever get emotionally involved? Cry? Laugh?

Hecuba—Priam's wife

The King and Queen question Rosencrantz and Guildenstern about their encounter with Hamlet. Polonius adds that Hamlet requests their presence at a play to be performed that night.

And you can not get from him why he puts on this confusion?

Did he receive you well?

He feels himself distracted, but from what cause he will not speak.

Yes, he received us well.

It so fell out that certain players that we passed on our way here were arriving at Elsinore and that seemed to bring him joy.

'Tis most true, and he beseeched me to entreat your Majesties to hear and see the matter.

With all my heart, it doth much content me to hear him so inclined.

Act III Scene i	The King excuses the Queen and reports that he and Polonius have set up a chance encounter between Ophelia and Hamlet (which they will observe) to determine whether Hamlet's insanity is caused by his love for Ophelia.

Sweet Gertrude, leave us, for we have sent for Hamlet, that he by accident may affront Ophelia— and her father and myself, unseen, may judge his affliction may be of his love or not.

I shall obey—and for your part Ophelia, I do wish that your good beauties be the happy cause of Hamlet's wildness and that your virtues will bring him to his senses.

Madam, I wish it may.

Ophelia walk you here and read this book, it will show how lonely you have been.

I hear him coming. Let's withdraw, my lord.

Think About It

At this point in the play, what is your opinion of Ophelia? Describe her positive qualities. After reading this section— what is the Queen's opinion of Ophelia?

Hamlet enters the scene obviously troubled about life. This is one of Shakespeare's most famous speeches—the "to be or not to be" speech.

Hamlet: To be or not to be—that is the question:
Whether 'tis nobler in the mind to suffer
The slings and arrows of outrageous fortune,
Or to take arms against a sea of troubles
And, by opposing, end them. To die, to sleep—
No more—and by a sleep to say we end
The heartache and the thousand natural shocks
That flesh is heir to—'tis a consummation
Devoutly to be wished. To die, to sleep—
To sleep perchance to dream. Ay, there's the **rub**,   **rub**—an obstacle
For in that sleep of death what dreams may come,
When we have shuffled off this mortal coil,
Must give us pause. There's the respect
That makes calamity of so long life.
For who would bear the whips and scorns of time,
Th'oppressor's wrong, the proud man's **contumely**,   **contumely**—contemptuous
The pangs of despised love, the law's delay,   treatment
The insolence of office, and the spurns
That patient merit of th'unworthy takes,
When he himself might his quietus make
With a bare **bodkin**? Who would **fardels** bear,   **bodkin**—a dagger without a sheath
To grunt and sweat under a weary life,   **fardels**—burdens
But that the dread of something after death,
The undiscovered country from whose bourn
No traveler returns, puzzles, the will
And makes us rather bear those ills we have
Than fly to others that we know not of?
Thus conscience does make cowards of us all,
And thus the native hue of resolution
Is sicklied o'er with the pale cast of thought,
And enterprises of great pitch and moment
With this regard their currents turn awry
And lose the name of action. —**Soft** you now,   **soft**—an exclamation meaning to
The fair Opehlia. —Nymph, in thy orisons   wait
Be all my sins remembered.

Hamlet greets Ophelia who states that she wants to return the gifts that he had given her. Hamlet denies giving them to her.

Good my lord, how does your Honor for this many a day?

I humbly thank you, well.

My lord, I have these remembrances of yours that I long to redeliver.

You did my lord, and with sweet words. Rich gifts wax poor when givers prove unkind. There my lord.

No, not I. I never gave you aught.

Get thee to a nunnery. Why wouldst thou be a breeder of sinners? If thou dost marry, I'll give thee this plague for thy dowry; be thou as chaste as ice, as pure as snow. Get thee to a nunnery, farewell. Or if thou wilt marry, marry a fool, for wise men know well enough what monsters you make of them. To a nunnery, go and quickly too. Farewell. I have heard of your paintings too—God hath given you one face and you make yourselves another. Go to—it hath made me mad. I say we will have no more marriage—those that are married already, all but one, shall live. The rest shall keep as they are. To a nunnery, go.

Heavenly powers, restore him! O, what a noble mind is here o'erthrown!

Think About It

A nunnery is a home and workplace for Catholic nuns. Explain why Hamlet would demand that Ophelia go there.

The King doubts that love is the source of Hamlet's madness and that he should be sent to England. Polonius suggests that Hamlet speak with his mother after the play and he will hide and listen.

King: Love? His affections do not that way tend;
Nor what he spake, though it lacked form a little,
Was not like madness. There's something in his soul
O'er which his melancholy sits on brood,
And I do doubt the hatch and the disclose
Will be some danger; which for to prevent,
I have in quick determination
Thus set it down; he shall with speed to England
For the demand of our neglected tribute.
Haply the seas, and countries different,
With variable objects, shall expel
This something-settled matter in his heart,
Whereon his brains still beating puts him thus
From fashion of himself. What think you on't?

Polonius: It shall do well. But yet do I believe
The origin and commencement of his grief
Sprung from neglected love.—How now, Ophelia?
You need not tell us what Lord Hamlet said;
We heard it all, —My lord, do as you please,
But, if you hold it fit, after the play
Let his queen-mother all alone entreat him
To show his grief. Let her be round with him;
And I'll be placed, so please you, in the ear
Of all their conference. If she find him not,
To England send him, or confine him where
Your wisdom best shall think.

King: It shall be so.
Madness in great ones must not unwatched go.

Think About It

The king seems to be quite worried about Hamlet. But at the same time does he appear to be suspicious? Reread the first four lines of this dialogue. What do you think?

Think About It

Polonius seems to believe that the origin of Hamlet's madness comes from his love of Ophelia. However, he also seems to think that Hamlet will confide in his mother. But explain why Polonius would want to hide in the room and eavesdrop on their conversation?

Hamlet instructs the players in their performance of the section of the play that he has written for them and he asks Horatio to watch his uncle, King Claudius' reaction to it.

Speak the speech, I pray you, as I pronounced it to you, trippingly on the tongue.

Yes, he received us well.

Do not saw the air too much with your hand, but use all gently.

Be not too tame neither, but let your own discretion be your tutor.

What ho, Horatio!

There is a play tonight before the King, one scene comes near the circumstance which I have told thee of my father's death. Observe my uncle and if his guilt do not itself unkennel in one speech, it is a damned ghost that we have seen.

Here, sweet lord, at your service—and if he escape whilst this play is playing, I will pay the theft.

Act III Scene ii	Members of the court arrive for the play. Before it begins, there is a "dumb show" or a scene without words imitating the murder scene—a king sleeping in a garden, a man entering and pouring poison in his ears, and then wooing the widowed Queen.

Enter a King and a Queen, (very lovingly) the Queen embracing him and he her. She kneels and makes a show of protestation unto him. He takes her up and declines his head upon her neck. He lies down upon a bank of flowers. She, seeing him asleep, leaves him. Soon, another man arrives, takes off the King's crown, kisses it, pours poison in the sleeper's ears, and leaves. The Queen returns, finds the King dead and makes passionate actions. The poisoner returns with three or four others and seems to condole her. The dead body is carried away. The poisoner woos the Queen with gifts. She seems harsh awhile, but in the end accepts his love.

Think About It

Put yourself in Claudius' position. You are ready to watch a play, when there is a "dumb show" that portrays the exact way that you murdered your brother. How do you react? Act guiltless and innocent—or panic and run?

miching in a dialect means sneaking; **mallecho** (malhecho) is Spanish for misdeed

The real play is performed and at the part when the King is poisoned in the garden, Claudius rises and runs out of the hall. Everyone follows, leaving Hamlet and Horatio together.

Rosencrantz and Guildenstern arrive to tell Hamlet that his mother wants to speak to him. Polonius arrives with the same message and all leave save for Hamlet. In a soliloquy he claims that he will be extremely honest with her.

The Queen, your mother, in great affliction of spirit, hat sent me to you.

She desires to speak with you.

We shall obey, were she ten times our mother.

My lord, the Queen would speak with you, and presently

Hamlet: 'Tis now the very witching time of night,
When churchyards yawn and hell itself breathes out
Contagion to this world. Now could I drink hot blood
And do such bitter business as the day
Would quake to look on. Soft, now to my mother.
O hear, lose not thy nature; let not ever
The soul of **Nero** enter this firm bosom.
Let me be cruel, not unnatural.
I will speak daggers to her, but une none.
My tongue and soul in this be hypocrites;
How in my words **somever** she be **shent**,
To give them **seals** never, my soul, consent.

Literary Term

This is an **allusion** to **Nero** a Roman emperor who set Rome on fire and murdered his mother Agrippina.

somever—however
shent—punished
seals—put words into action

Think About It

If you were Hamlet's mother and had just witnessed the disturbing events of the play—what would you have to say to your son? Would you be understanding, frightened, or angry?

The King, believing Hamlet to be dangerous, asks Rosencrantz and Guildenstern to escort Hamlet to England. Polonius reminds the King of his plan to eavesdrop on the Queen and Hamlet.

I like not the way he acts, nor is it safe to let his madness range. Prepare to escort him to England. Arm you, I pray you, this speedy voyage.

We will haste us.

We will provide to keep those bodies safe that live and feed upon your Majesty.

My lord, he's going to his mother's closet, behind the arras I will hide, and listen. I'll call upon you ere you go to bed and tell you what I know.

Thanks, dear my lord.

**Act III
Scene iii**

In a soliloquy, the King confesses his guilt and admits his desire for power remains; he kneels down to pray.

King: O, my offense is rank, it smells to heaven;
It hath the primal eldest curse upon't,
A brother's murder. Pray can I not,
Though inclination be as sharp as will.
My stronger guilt defeats my strong intent,
And, like a man to double business bound,
I stand in pause where I shall first begin
And both neglect. What if this cursed hand
Were thicker than itself with brother's blood?
Is there not rain enough in the sweet heavens
To **wash it white as snow**? Whereto serves mercy
But to confront the visage of offense?
And what's in prayer but this twofold force,
To be forestallèd ere we come to fall,
Or pardoned being down? Then I'll look up.
My fault is past. But, O, what form of prayer
Can serve my turn? "Forgive me my foul murder"?
That cannot be, since I am still possessed
Of those effects for which I did the murder;
My crown, mine own ambition, and my queen.
May one be pardoned and retain th'offense?
In the corrupted currents of this world,
Offense's gilded hand may shove by justice,
And oft 'tis seen the wicked prize itself
Buys out the law. But 'tis not so above:
There is no shuffling; there the action lies
In his true nature, and we ourselves compelled,
Even to the teeth and forehead of our faults,
To give in evidence. What then? What rests?
Try what repentance can. What can it not?
Yet what can it, when one cannot repent?
O wretched state! O bosom black as death!
O limèd soul, that, struggling to be free,
Art more engaged! Help, angels! Make assay.
Bow, stubborn knees, and heart with strings of steel
Be soft as sinews of the newborn babe.
All may be well.

Literary Term

The use of a **simile** to describe the King's desire to wash himself of the guilt "as white as snow" brings dynamic imagery to the passage and makes it come alive.

Think About It

The King seems to be struggling with his conscience. He wants to be forgiven for his crime, but yet he longs to retain the power of the crown and the queen. Do you believe that the King is sorry or is he sending mixed messages?

Hamlet on his way to see his mother passes the King praying and draws his sword.

Hamlet: Now I might do it, now he is a-praying,
And now I'll do't
And so he goes to heaven,
And so am I revenged. That would be scanned;
A villain kills my father, and for that,
I, his sole son, do this same villain send
To heaven.
Why, this is hire and salary, not revenge.
He took my father grossly, full of bread,
With all his crimes broad blown, as flush as May;
And how his audit stands who knows save heaven.
But in our circumstance and course of thought
'tis havy with him. And am I then revenged
To take him in the purging of his soul,
When he is fit and seasoned for his passage?
No.
Up sword, and know thou a more horrid hent
         (He sheathes his sword)
When he is drunk asleep, or in his rage,
Or in th'incestuous pleasure of his bed,
At game a-swearing, or about some act
That has no relish of salvation in't—
Then trip him, that his heels may kick at heaven,
And that his soul may be damned and black
As hell, whereto it goes. My mother stays.
This physic but prolongs thy sickly days.

Think About It

if Hamlet kills his uncle while he is praying, his soul, according to religious beliefs, will go to heaven. Hamlet has a perfect opportunity to revenge his father's death. Do you agree with Hamlet's decision? Explain your answer.

Hamlet greets his mother who is frightened by his aggressive behavior and cries out. Polonius, hiding behind the tapestry, echoes her call, and Hamlet, thinking that it is Claudius, stabs him through the fabric.

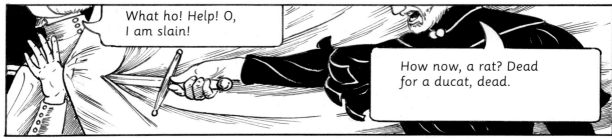

Hamlet continues his angry rage against his mother and questions how she could marry such as man as Claudius.

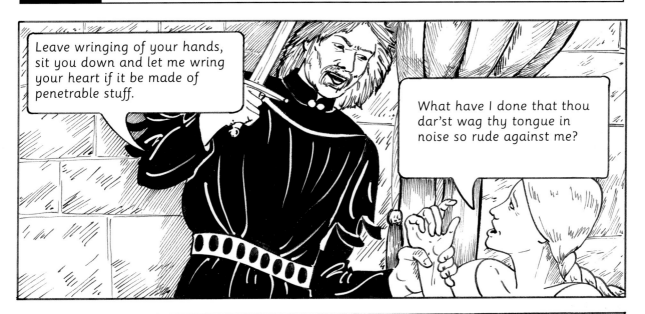

Leave wringing of your hands, sit you down and let me wring your heart if it be made of penetrable stuff.

What have I done that thou dar'st wag thy tongue in noise so rude against me?

Have you eyes? Look at your husband, like a mildewed ear—you cannot call it love—he's a murderer, a villain, a **cutpurse of the empire and the rule**.

O, speak to me no more! These words like daggers enter in my ears. No more, sweet Hamlet.

Think About It

Hamlet is flinging insults about his uncle—"**a cutpurse of the empire and the rule**" is one of many. A "cutpurse" is a thief—is Hamlet correct in calling his uncle a thief in this context?

45

**Act III
Scene iv**

Suddenly the Ghost appears. Hamlet can see it, but his mother cannot. The ghost reminds Hamlet of his duty to revenge his death.

Do you come to chide your tardy son, that lapsed in acting upon your command?

This visitation is to remind you of your almost blunted purpose. But, look to your mother, step between her and her fighting soul.

Alas, he's mad.

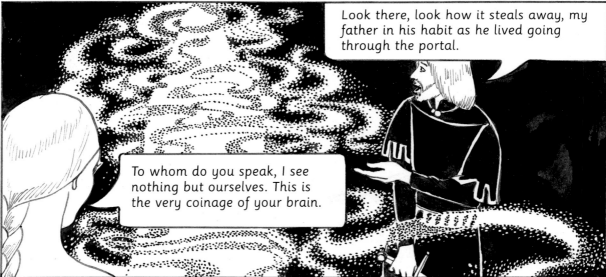

Look there, look how it steals away, my father in his habit as he lived going through the portal.

To whom do you speak, I see nothing but ourselves. This is the very coinage of your brain.

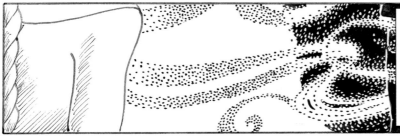

Think About It

What are your thoughts about Gertrude? Do you believe that she is innocent, or did she take part in the planning of King Hamlet's death?

Hamlet explains to his mother that he is only pretending to be mad and he asks that she does not reveal this to his uncle. He reminds his mother that he is being sent to England.

> I essentially am not in madness, but mad in craft. With this in secrecy, do not let the birds fly.

> Be thou assure, if words be made of breath and breath of life, I have no life to breathe what thou hast said to me.

> I must to England, you know that.

> Alack, I had forgot! 'Tis so concluded on.

> There's letters sealed; and my two schoolfellows bear the mandate and they must sweep my way and **marshal me to knavery**. This man shall set me packing.

Think About It

Hamlet's friends, Rosencrantz and Guildenstern are taking him to England with sealed letters. What do you think is written inside? Do you think Hamlet knows? Does the line **"marshal me to knavery"** give you a hint?

Hamlet says goodnight to his mother and drags the body of Polonius away.

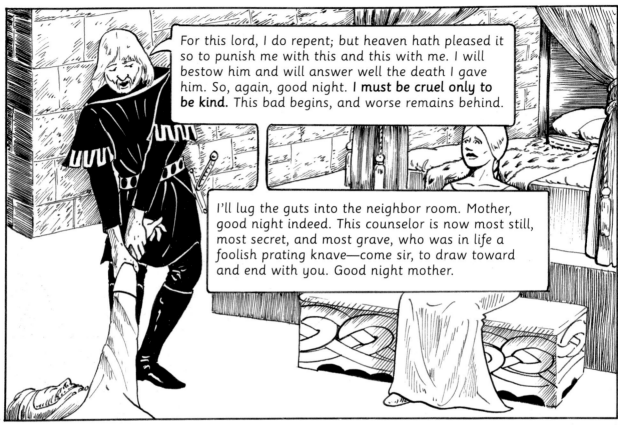

For this lord, I do repent; but heaven hath pleased it so to punish me with this and this with me. I will bestow him and will answer well the death I gave him. So, again, good night. **I must be cruel only to be kind.** This bad begins, and worse remains behind.

I'll lug the guts into the neighbor room. Mother, good night indeed. This counselor is now most still, most secret, and most grave, who was in life a foolish prating knave—come sir, to draw toward and end with you. Good night mother.

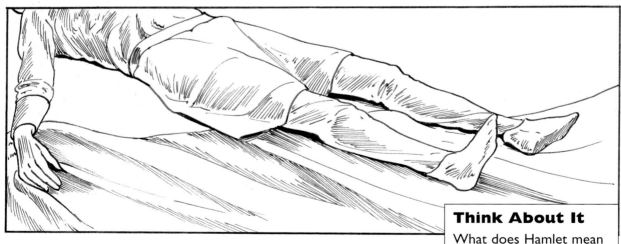

Think About It

What does Hamlet mean when he says "**I must be cruel only to be kind**"?

Queen Gertrude tells Claudius about Hamlet and the murder of Polonius. He sends Rosencrantz and Guildenstern to find Hamlet and to recover the body.

There's matter in these sighs, help us understand them.

Ah, what have I seen tonight! Hamlet is **mad as the sea and wind when both contend which is the mightier**. He hath killed a good old man, Polonius.

Oh, heavy deed! O Gertrude, come away! The sun no sooner shall the mountains touch, but we will ship him hence and this vile deed we must with all our majesty and skill excuse.

Friends both, go seek Hamlet out, speak fair, and bring the body to the chapel. I pray you haste in this.

Literary Term

A **simile** is used to describe Hamlet's madness—as "**mad as the sea and wind when both contend which is the mightier**."

Rosencrantz and Guildenstern ask Hamlet for the body of Polonius, but he appears to act bizarrely and refuses to tell them where it is.

Safely stowed. But soft, what noise? Who calls on Hamlet? Oh, here they come.

Tell us where 'tis, that we may take it to the chapel.

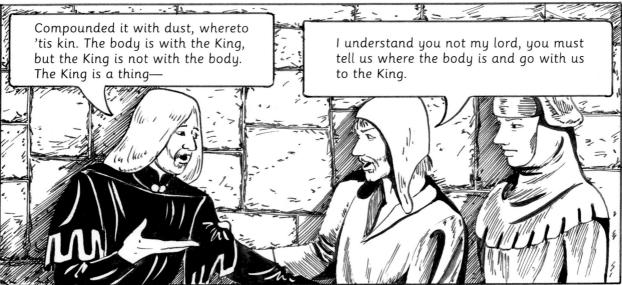

Compounded it with dust, whereto 'tis kin. The body is with the King, but the King is not with the body. The King is a thing—

I understand you not my lord, you must tell us where the body is and go with us to the King.

Think About It

What do you think Hamlet is up to? He told his mother that he was merely acting like he was mad, but do you think there is more to it now?

The King asks Hamlet where the body is and Hamlet responds in a silly manner. Instructing Hamlet to leave immediately for England, he reveals in a soliloquy that Hamlet will be killed when he arrives.

King: Now, Hamlet, where's Polonius?

Hamlet: At supper.

King: At supper where?

Hamlet: Not where he eats, but where he is eaten.
A certain convocation of politic worms are e'en at him.
Your worm is your only emperor for diet.
We fat all creatures else to fat us, and we fat ourselves
for maggots. Your fat king and your lean beggar is but
variable service—two dishes but to one table. That's the end.

King: Where is Polonius?

Hamlet: In heaven. Send thither to see. If your messenger
find him not there, seek him i'th'other place yourself.
But if, indeed, you find him not within this month,
you shall nose him as you go up the stairs into the lobby.

King: Hamlet, this deed, for thine especial safety, must
we send thee hence with fiery quickness. Therefore prepare
thyself. The **bark** is ready, and the wind at help,
Th' associates tend and everything is bent for England.

bark—ship

Hamlet: For England, good. I see a cherub that sees them.
But come, for England. Farewell, dear mother.
                    He exits

King: Follow him at foot; tempt him with speed aboard.
Delay it not. I'll have him hence tonight.
Away, for everything else is sealed and done.
                    All but the King exit

And England, if my love thou hold'st at aught
Thou mayst not coldly set
Our sovereign process, which imports at full,
By letters congruing to that effect,
The present death of Hamlet. Do it, England;
For like the hectic in my blood he rages,
**And thou must cure me. Till I know 'tis done,
Howe'er my haps, my joys were ne'er begun.**

Literary Term
Shakespeare often uses a
rhyming couplet to end a
scene. The last two lines of
this soliloquy are a rhyming
couplet—or, two lines that
rhyme.

On the way to the ship, Hamlet meets the Norwegian captain of young Fortinbras' army. Hamlet is inspired by Fortinbras' desire to fight for something as insignificant as a plot of land.

Go, Captain, greet the Danish king and ask for permission to march over his kingdom.

I will do't, my lord.

Good sir, whose powers are these?

The nephew to old Norway.

How purposed sir, I pray you.

Truly to speak, we go to gain a little patch of ground that hath no profit but the name. I would not farm it, nor would it yield to Norway or the Pole.

I do not know why yet I live to say "This thing's to do"—I have cause, will, strength and means to do it. Examples gross as earth exhort me: Witness this army of such mass and charge, led by a prince with divine ambition. How stand I then with a father killed, a mother stained. **O, from this time forth, my thoughts be bloody or be nothing worth!**

Think About It

Reread the last line of Hamlet's soliloquy—how has he changed over the past few scenes?

The King and Queen speak with Ophelia who sings strange songs and seems incoherent and insane. Ophelia's brother Laertes arrives.

How now, Ophelia? Alas sweet lady, what imports this song?

How do you, pretty lady? How long hath she been like this? Follow her close, give her good watch, I pray you.

"How should I your true love know from another one? By his cockle hat and staff and his sandal shoon...."

Give me my father!

Why art thou thus incensed?

Laertes shall be king! Laertes king!

Calmly, good Laertes.

Think About It

The King and Queen seem unaffected by Laertes' anger. How would you explain their behavior?

Laertes, obviously disturbed, declares that he will seek revenge for his father's death. Ophelia enters and Laertes is heartbroken when he sees that she has gone mad.

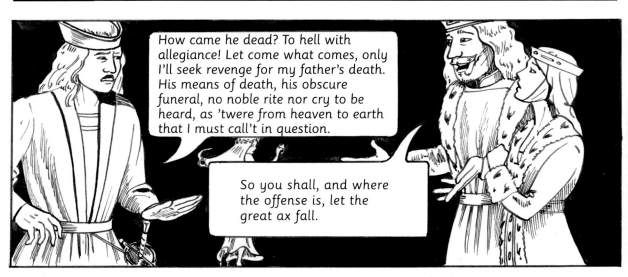

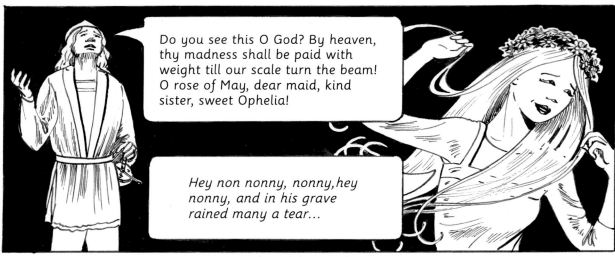

Think About It

What is going on with Ophelia? Why is she acting so strangely? Explain all of the events that have occurred in Ophelia's life recently. How do these events help explain her present frame of mind?

Sailors deliver a letter to Horatio from Hamlet about his return to Denmark onboard a pirate ship.

Horatio, when thou shalt have overlooked this, give these fellows some means to the King. They have letters for him. Ere we were two days old at sea, a pirate of very warlike appointment gave us chase. Finding ourselves too slow of sail, we put on a compelled valor, and in the grapple I boarded them. On the instant, they got clear of our ship; so I alone became their prisoner. They have dealt with me like thieves of mercy, but they knew what they did: I am to do a good turn for them. Let the King have the letters I have sent, and repair thou to me with as much speed as thou wouldst fly death. I have words to speak in thine ear will make thee dumb; yet are they much too light for the bore of the matter. These good fellows will bring thee where I am. Rosencrantz and Guildenstern hold their course for England; of them I have much to tell thee. Farewell.

     He that thou knowest thine,

         Hamlet

Think About It

Imagine being captured by pirates and then being returned to your homeland in exchange for a "good turn." What might they ask of Hamlet?

The King explains to Laertes the reasons he did not bury Polonius in a proper ceremony. A messenger arrives with a letter from Hamlet, stating that he is returning to Denmark alone.

For two special reasons in denying your father a funeral: the Queen, his mother lives almost by his looks and the great love the general public bear him.

And so have I a noble father lost, and a sister driven into desperate terms. But my revenge will come.

Letters, my lord, from Hamlet. These to your Majesty, this to the Queen. Brought in by sailors, my lord.

It says that he is returning tomorrow, alone. What should this mean? Are all the rest come back? Or is it some abuse and no such thing?

I am lost in it, but let him come, it warms the sickness in my heart.

We will double varnish the praise of your swordsmanship and wager on your heads. And, with little shuffling, requite him for your father.

I will do it and for that purpose I'll anoint my sword with a poison so deadly, nothing under the moon can save the thing from death.

Let's further think of this. If this should fail, I'll have prepared him a chalice should he by chance escape your venomed sword, our purpose my hold there.

Think About It

What are back-up plans? Have you ever made additional plans for an event just in case the original plan didn't work out? Are these back-up plans a good idea or merely a waste of time?

The Queen arrives with news that Laertes' sister Ophelia has drowned.

One woe doth tread upon another's heel, so fast they follow. Your sister's drowned.

Drowned? O, where?

There is a willow near the brook, there she made garlands for her hair and fell in the weeping brook till her garments, heavy with their drink, pulled the poor wretch from her melodious lay, to muddy death.

Too much of water hast thou poor Ophelia, and therefore I forbid my tears. Adieu, my lord. I have a speech o'fire that fain would blaze, but that this folly drowns it.

Think About It

Reread Laertes' response to his sister's death: "Too much of water has thou poor Ophelia, and therefore I forbid my tears." Describe what he might be going through emotionally right now that would explain this type of response.

<table>
<tr><td>**Act V
Scene i**</td><td>A gravedigger and a companion discuss the burial of Ophelia.
Hamlet and Horatio observe the digging and reminisce about a
skull.</td></tr>
</table>

> Is she to be buried in Christian burial, when she willfully seeks her own salvation?

> I tell thee she is. Therefore make her grave straightway—the coroner's inquest finds it to be Christian.

> This same skull was Yorick's skull, the King's jester.

> This? Let me see. Alas poor Yorick! I knew him Horatio—a fellow of infinite jest, of most excellent fancy. He hath bore me on his back a thousand times.

Think About It

The gravediggers are questioning the fact that Ophelia is being buried in a churchyard because according to religious doctrine, those who commit suicide are not entitled to a Christian burial. What are your thoughts on this doctrine?

Think About It Again

Hamlet, holding the skull of his father's court jester—someone hired to entertain the King—fondly remembers an old friend. How does this show yet another side of Hamlet's personality?

At the site of the funeral, Laertes is distraught and sees Hamlet. The two get into a scuffle, but Hamlet declares his love for Ophelia.

60

After an angry torrent of words directed at Laertes, Hamlet leaves and the King sends Horatio after him. The King reminds Laertes of their conversation the previous night.

Swounds, show me what thou to do. Weep, fight, fast, tear thyself, drink up **eisel**, eat a crocodile? I'll do it.

I pray thee, good Horatio, wait upon him.

Strengthen your patience in our last night's speech; we'll put the matter to the present push.

eisel—vinegar

**Act V
Scene ii**

At the castle, Hamlet tells Horatio of the discovery he made en route to England.

In my heart there was a kind of fighting that would not let me sleep. So, up from my cabin in the dark groped I to find out and fingered their packet and went back to my room. In unfolding their commission, I found a royal knavery, an exact command that upon my arrival in England, my head should be struck off.

Is it possible?

But wilt thou hear how I proceed? I sat down and wrote a new commission, stating that the bearers of this be put to sudden death and having my father's signet in my purse, a model of the Danish seal, I folded it and sealed it and returned it to its original position. Now the next day was our sea-fight and what to this was sequent thou knowest already.

So Guildenstern and Rosencrantz go to't. Why what a king is this!

Think About It

What would your reaction be if you discovered that your stepfather/uncle plotted against you and that your two best friends betrayed you in accepting the commission? Did Rosencrantz and Guildenstern know about what was in the letter when they accepted the assignment?

<table>
<tr><td>

**Act V
Scene ii**

</td><td>

A young courtier named Osric arrives to announce that King Claudius has asked that Hamlet fence (swordfight) with Laertes. Horatio fears that Hamlet will lose.

</td></tr>
</table>

Welcome back to Denmark, I should impart a thing to you from his Majesty.

I humbly thank you sir.

His Majesty bade me signify to you that he has laid a great wager on your head.

I will receive it, with all diligence of spirit.

Horatio: You will lose, my lord.

Hamlet: I do not think so. Since he went into France, I have been in continual practice. I shall win at the odds; but thou wouldst not think how ill all's here about my heart. But it is no matter.

Horatio: Nay, good my lord—

Hamlet: It is but foolery, but it is such a kind of **gaingiving** as would perhaps trouble a woman.

Horatio: If your mind dislike anything, obey it. I will forestall their repair hither and say you are not fit.

Hamlet: No a whit. We defy **augury**. There is **a special providence in the fall of a sparrow**. If it be now, 'tis not to come; if it be not to come, it will be now; if it be not now, yet it will come. The readiness is all. Since no man of aught he leaves knows, what is't to leave betimes? Let be.

Literary Term

An **allusion** is used here—*a special providence in the fall of a sparrow* refers to a passage in the Bible— which was one writing that many during Shakespeare's time would understand. Matthew 10: 29–31, which states do not be afraid of those who kill the body but cannot kill the soul, be afraid of one who can kill both the body and the soul. "Are not two sparrows sold for a penny? Yet not one of them will fall to the ground apart from the will of your Father. And even the very hairs of your head are all numbered. So don't be afraid you are worth more than many sparrows."

---

gaingiving—misgiving
augury—the art of prophesizing or telling the future

Just before the fencing begins, the King asks Hamlet to shake Laertes' hand and Hamlet apologizes to him.

Come, Hamlet, come and take this hand from me.

Give me your pardon, sir. I have done you wrong; but pardon it as you are a gentleman. I proclaim it was my madness, and let my disclaiming from a purposed evil free me so far in your most generous thoughts and that I have shot my arrow over the house and hurt my brother.

I will no reconcilement make till some elder masters of known honor voice to keep my name ungored, but until then I do receive your offered love like love and will not wrong it.

Think About It

Hamlet offers his apologies to Laertes, and blames it on his madness. What are your thoughts about the "Madness" argument now? Is he or isn't he—was he or wasn't Hamlet mad?

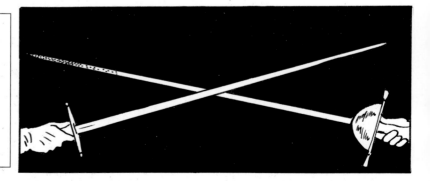

The King has the goblets of wine placed on the table, Laertes and Hamlet play and the Queen drinks from the poisoned cup.

King: Set me the stoups of wine upon that table.
If Hamlet give the first or second hit
Or quit in answer of the third exchange,
Let all the battlements their ordnance fire.
The King shall drink to Hamlet's better breath,
And in the cup an union shall he throw,
Richer than that which four successive kings
In Denmark's crown have worn. Give me the cups,
An let the kettle to the trumpet speak,
The trumpet to the cannoneer with out,
The cannons to the heavens, the heaven to earth,
"Now the King drinks to Hamlet." Come, begin.
And you, the judges, bear a wary eye.

Stay, give me drink—Hamlet, this pearl is thine.
Here's to thy health.
(He drinks and drops the pearl in the cup)

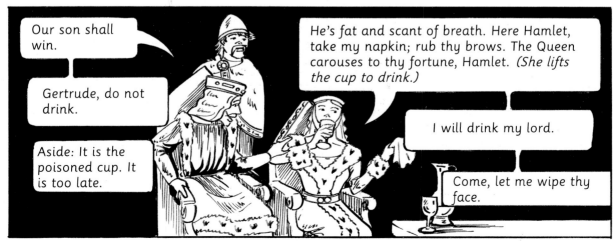

Our son shall win.

Gertrude, do not drink.

Aside: It is the poisoned cup. It is too late.

He's fat and scant of breath. Here Hamlet, take my napkin; rub thy brows. The Queen carouses to thy fortune, Hamlet. *(She lifts the cup to drink.)*

I will drink my lord.

Come, let me wipe thy face.

| **Act V Scene ii** | Laertes wounds Hamlet with the poisoned sword, and in scuffling, they accidentally exchange swords and Hamlet wounds Laertes with the same poisoned sword. The Queen dies. |

Look to the Queen there, ho!

She swoons to see them bleed.

No, no, the drink, the drink! O, my dear Hamlet! The drink! I am poisoned.

O villainy! Let the door be locked. Treachery! Seek it out.

Think About It

What do you think is going to happen next? The Queen is dead; Laertes and Hamlet have both been stabbed with a poisoned sword—what else could possibly happen?

Before he dies, Laertes tells Hamlet that the King is to blame for all of the deaths and exchanges forgiveness with him. Hamlet stabs the King and forces him to drink the poisoned wine.

The treachery is here, the envenomed instrument is in thy hand. The King, the King's to blame.

Defend me friends! I am but hurt.

The point envenomed too! Then, venom, to thy work.

Here, thou incestuous, murderous damned Dane, Drink off this potion. Is thy union here?

He is justly served. It is a poison tempered by himself. Exchange forgiveness with me—mine and my father's death come not upon thee, nor yours on me.

**Act V
Scene ii**

Hamlet speaks to Horatio and before dying, transfers the crown to young Fortinbras who has just arrived.

Hamlet: Heaven make thee free of it. I follow thee.—
I am dead, Horatio.—Wretched queen, adieu.—
You that look pale and tremble at this chance,
That are but mutes or audience to this act,
Had I but time (as this fell sergeant, Death,
Is strict in his arrest), O, I could tell you—
But let it be.—Horatio, I am dead.
Thou livest; report me and my cause aright
To the unsatisfied.

Horatio: Never believe it
I am more antique Roman than a Dane.
Here's yet some liquor left. *[He picks up the wine goblet]*

Hamlet: As thou'rt a man,
Give me the cup. Let go! By heaven, I'll ha't.
O God, Horatio what a wounded name,
Things standing thus unknown, shall I leave behind me!
If thou didst ever hold me in thy heart,
Absent thee from felicity awhile
And in this harsh world draw thy breath in pain
To tell my story.   *[The sound of marching and a shot within]*
      What warlike noise is this?

Osric: Young Fortinbras, with conquest come from Poland,
To th'ambassadors of England gives
This warlike volley.

Hamlet: O, I die, Horatio!
The potent poison quite o'ercrows my spirit.
I cannot live to hear the news from England.
But I do prophesy th'election lights
On Fortinbras; he has my dying voice.
So tell him, with th'occurrents, more and less,
Which have solicited—the rest is silence.
O, O, O, O,   *[Hamlet dies]*

Horatio: Now cracks a noble heart. Good night, sweet prince,
And flights of angels sing thee to thy rest.

> **Think About It**
> Looking back over the play, how many people have died during the course of the five acts? Remember King Hamlet was already dead when the play began.

<table>
<tr><td>**Act V
Scene ii**</td><td>Fortinbras enters as do the ambassadors from England. Horatio reports that he will explain the events and Fortinbras declares that Hamlet shall have a military funeral.</td></tr>
</table>

What sight is this? That thou so many princes at a shot so bloodily hast struck?

What is it you would see? If it be of woe and wonder, cease your search.

The site is dismal, and our affairs from England come too late to tell him that Rosencrantz and Guildenstern are dead.

How these things came about, you shall hear—of carnal, bloody, and unnatural acts, of casual slaughters…all this can I truly deliver.

Let us haste to hear it and for me with sorrow I embrace my fortune and rights of memory in this kingdom. Carry Hamlet to the stage, for he was likely to have proved most royal. For his passage, the soldier's music and the rite of war speak loudly for him.

Think About It

Adding Rosencrantz and Guildenstern to the number that has died, how many do you count? This is what tragedies are about—death. Hamlet is now ended. Fortinbras has revenged his father's death, but were you expecting that it would be so easy for him?

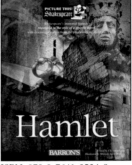
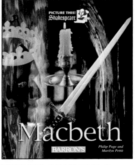

At last! Shakespeare in Language everyone can understand...

SHAKESPEARE MADE EASY Series

Scene 7

*Macbeth's castle. Enter a **sewer** directing divers servants. Then enter **Macbeth**.*

Macbeth If it were done, when 'tis done, then 'twere well
It were done quickly: if th' assassination
Could trammel up the consequence, and catch,
With his surcease, success; that but this blow
5 Might be the be-all and the end-all here,
But here, upon this bank and shoal of time,
We'd jump the life to come. But in these cases
We still have judgement here: that we but teach
Blood instructions, which being taught return
10 To plague th'inventor: this even-handed justice
Commends th'ingredience of our poisoned chalice
To our own lips. He's here in double trust:
First, as I am his kinsman and his subject,
Strong both against the deed: then, as his host,
15 Who should against his murderer shut the door,
Not bear the knife myself. Besides, this Duncan
Hath borne his faculties so meek, hath been
So clear in his great office, that his virtues
Will plead like angels, trumpet-tounged, against
20 The deep damnation of his taking-off;
And pity, like a naked new-born babe,
Striding the blast, or Heaven's cherubin, horsed
Upon the sightless couriers of the air,
Shall blow the horrid deed in every eye,
25 That tears shall drown the wind. I have no spur
To prick the sides of my intent, but only
Vaulting ambition, which o'erleaps itself,
And falls on th'other –

Scene 7

*A room in **Macbeth's** castle. A **Butler** and several **Waiters** cross, carrying dishes of food. Then **Macbeth** enters. He is thinking about the proposed murder of **King Duncan**.*

Macbeth If we could get away with the deed after it's done, then the quicker it were done, the better. If the murder had no consequences, and his death ensured success...If, when I strike the blow, that would be the end of it – here, right here, on this side of eternity – we'd willingly chance the life to come. But usually, we get what's coming to us here on earth. We teach the art of bloodshed, then become the victims of our own lessons. This evenhanded justice makes us swallow our own poison. [*Pause*] Duncan is here on double trust: first, because I'm his kinsman and his subject (both good arguments against the deed); then, because I'm his host, who should protect him from his murderer—not bear the knife. Besides, this Duncan has used his power so gently, he's been so incorruptible his great office, that his virtues will plead like angels, their tongues trumpeting the damnable horror of his murder. And pity, like a naked newborn babe or Heaven's avenging angels riding the winds, will cry the deed to everyone so that tears will blind the eye. I've nothing to spur me on but high-leaping ambition, which can often bring about one's downfall.

Shakespeare is Made Easy for these titles:

Available at your local book store or visit
www.barronseduc.com

A simplified modern translation appears side-by-side with the original Elizabethan text...plus there's helpful background material, study questions, and other aids to better grades.

Yes, up-to-date language now makes it easier to score well on tests *and* enjoy the ageless beauty of the master's works.

Barron's Educational Series, Inc.
250 Wireless Blvd.
Hauppauge, N.Y. 11788
Order toll-free: 1-800-645-3476
Order by fax: 1-631-434-3217

Prices subject to change without notice.

In Canada:
Georgetown Book Warehouse
34 Armstrong Ave.
Georgetown, Ontario L7G 4R9
Canadian orders: 1-800-247-7160
Order by fax: 1-800-887-1594

Each book: paperback
NCR = No Canadian Rights

(#16) R 1/14

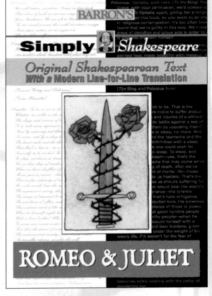